Original title:
The Ocean's Paradise

Copyright © 2025 Creative Arts Management OÜ
All rights reserved.

Author: Jameson Hartfield
ISBN HARDBACK: 978-1-80581-603-4
ISBN PAPERBACK: 978-1-80581-130-5
ISBN EBOOK: 978-1-80581-603-4

Celestial Seas

In the waves, fish wear ties,
With seaweed wraps, they criticize.
Crabs dance like they own the floor,
Shouting, 'Who could ask for more?'

Starfish lounge with sunglasses on,
Making sure their tans go strong.
Seagulls squawk, they think they're suave,
While dolphins giggle, quite the trove!

A Dance of Driftwood

Driftwood stars in a ballet show,
Twisting and turning, a proper pro.
Seashells clap with a conch-shell cheer,
Who knew such talent lived down here?

A jellyfish sings a high-pitched tune,
While crabs fight over a bright blue balloon.
The ocean floor is a quirky stage,
Ethel the eel steals the show—what a rage!

Beneath the Surface

Beneath the waves, there's quite a ball,
Octopuses juggle, not a single fall.
Clownfish giggle, they're in on the joke,
As bubbles rise up, it's a bubbly smoke.

Deep-sea monsters, they throw a bash,
With plankton punch and a seaweed splash.
But careful with the light, folks, it's a trap—
Flashlights turn them into fishy scrap!

Salty Serenity

In the salty foam, mermaids prance,
With such wild flair, they take a chance.
They comb their hair with forks from the shore,
While laughing at sailors who can't find their oar.

A sea turtle hosts a poker night,
With fishy chips that are quite a sight.
But when it's time to deal the cards,
It's a game of 'who can withstand the shards!'

Windswept Shores of Solitude

Seagulls squawk like they own the place,
Sand gets stuck in every little space.
A crab in a tux, with a dapper claw,
Waves crash, he bows, it's quite the law.

Beach chairs dance in the salty breeze,
While sunscreen battles ants with ease.
A fish flips me off as I stroll by,
It's the beach life, oh me, oh my!

Reflections in the Sea Glass

I found a bottle, it had a note,
It said, 'Your sandwich? I ate the whole Oat!'
Reflecting on life through fragments bright,
This sea glass world feels just right.

A starfish sings, trying to win a prize,
With seaweed hair covering its eyes.
Jellyfish giggle, float about with glee,
In this wacky world, it's just you and me.

Adrift in a Sea of Wonder

A floatie dog begs for a sunken toy,
While I attempt surfing, oh what a ploy!
Tangled in noodles, oh what a sight,
I scream like a seagull, just take flight!

Mussels form a band, playing on rocks,
While I chase a wave, wearing mismatched socks.
The ocean's a circus, a splashy affair,
It tickles my toes and messes my hair!

Glistening Treasures of the Coast

Shells tell stories of fishy pranks,
While crabs hold meetings, forming their ranks.
Lost in the treasure of glitter and foam,
This sandy oasis feels like home.

Octopuses juggle with eight nimble arms,
Dolphins are diving, showcasing charms.
When waves giggle, the world feels bright,
In this kooky bay, everything's all right!

Moonlit Secrets Beneath the Surface

The fish have parties, who knew?
They dance with seaweed in a hue.
A crab in a tux, feeling quite grand,
Sipping on bubbles while taking a stand.

The jellyfish glow like disco lights,
While octopuses host karaoke nights.
With laughter and splashes, the night gets wild,
And every mermaid there is just a child.

A Symphony of Waves

The waves tap dance upon the shore,
With seagulls laughing, asking for more.
A clam sings out, with style and grace,
While starfish twirl, showing off their face.

The tide plays music, with shells as drums,
While crabs in bow ties look dapper and dumb.
A dolphin juggles while fish keep score,
It's a concert of chaos, who could ask for more?

Sun-Kissed Memories on the Shore

I built a sandcastle, oh what a sight,
But a seagull swooped in for a bite!
My moat filled with water, it looked so nice,
Till a kid splashed in—oh, isn't that nice?

Beach umbrellas like mushrooms so bright,
They all wiggle when the wind is just right.
I think that crab wants to steal my flip-flop,
But wait, let it happen—this is pure pop!

Depths of a Tranquil Heart

In peaceful depths where fish do play,
A little goldfish has something to say.
With bubbles rising, it giggles and spins,
In serene silence where fun truly begins.

A sea turtle, wise with a humorous grin,
Says, "Slow down, my friend, let the laughter begin."
With corals and trinkets to make you feel light,
Dive into joy, it's an amusing sight!

Nautical Enchantment

A seagull stole my sandwich, oh dear!
It swooped down fast, I let out a cheer.
With salty winds and waves so spry,
I waved goodbye as it soared high.

Crabs wear hats and dance a jig,
While fish play cards, it's quite a gig.
The octopus serves drinks with glee,
And offers chips – oh, not for free!

Sunlit Vistas

Under sunbeams, the beach balls bounce,
A toddler's laughter, a giant flounce.
The sunscreen war – it's quite a sight,
With slippery slides in the daylight.

A dolphin's joke got the crowd to snort,
As waves came in like a playful sport.
Flip-flops flying, umbrellas too,
Beach day chaos – oh, what a view!

Harbor of Harmony

At the dock, the ducks unite,
With quacks and quibbles, what a sight!
They float on by, with a sassy stroke,
One spilled the tea, and laughter woke.

A pirate's parrot sings off-key,
While crabs form bands worth a fee.
An anchor's caught, in tangled lines,
But the fish just giggle, sipping brine.

Floating on Blue

The lazy waves, they tease and sway,
While sun hats dance on a sunny bay.
Jellyfish joke, in shimmering hues,
Making waves with their silly moves.

Surfers tumble, then strike a pose,
Splashing around, who really knows?
Each ripple hides a sneaky grin,
Where laughter blooms beneath the din.

Nautical Whispers and Mermaid Tales

Bubbles rise, fish giggle, swim with glee,
A crab in shades, playing beach frisbee.
Octopuses argue, who's the best dancer,
While shrimp tell jokes, drop a true romancer.

Seagulls squawk in wigs, on the shore to parade,
Clams tap their feet in a glorious charade.
Jellyfish juggle, what a sight to see,
No one told the starfish, 'you can't climb a tree!'

Walruses waltz, twirling around with flair,
As dolphins dive deep, flipping without a care.
The tide hums a tune, a melody of cheers,
In this quirky realm, there are no worries or fears.

So come join the fun, leave your troubles behind,
In this silly spectacle, joy's what you'll find.
With laughter and mirth, we'll make quite a tale,
Living in harmony, with frolicsome scale.

Starlit Shores of Reflection

Under moonlight beams, the sand crabs are prancing,
Seashells are singing, oh, they know how to be dancing.
Turtles on scooters, zooming with delight,
While fish in bow ties finesse the night.

Starfish hold meetings, vote for best-dressed,
A crab critiques, while his mate's unimpressed.
Seagulls gossip, spinning stories of sand,
Every tale a treasure, just a few grains at hand.

The echoing waves chuckle, rolling with style,
As plankton play poker, laughing all the while.
Mermaids debate on who's got the best fins,
While dolphins lend laughter as the party begins.

So come, bring your giggles, let them unleash,
Where sunsets paint smiles and joy won't cease.
In this world of whimsy, we'll float and we'll sway,
In starlit reflections, we'll dance the night away.

Scenic Serenity

Seashells cracked under my feet,
As crabs scuttle, they feel the heat.
The seagulls squawk, they've lost their way,
While I just laugh and twirl and sway.

A dolphin leaps, what a silly blur,
In my flip-flops, I start to stir.
The tide rolls in, my drink takes a dip,
I yell, "Hey buddy, don't take my sip!"

Odyssey of the Waves

A boat named 'Oops' skips on the brine,
Captain's compass? Nah, I'm fine!
The gusty wind pulls my hat right off,
With hair a mess, I break out in scoff.

A splash from behind, it's Fido the fish,
Who dreams of barking – that's his wish!
The beach ball flies, it hits me smack,
I'm chasing fun, no turning back!

Crescendo of the Currents

Waves crash loud like a rock band's song,
I jump and dance, can't do it wrong.
A mermaid waves, with a gelatin jig,
But I just slip and do the crab dig.

Sandy toes and giggles abound,
The tide pulls back, my shoe's not found.
"Catch me if you can!" I shout with glee,
While the fish roll their eyes at me!

Allure of the Abyss

What's lurking down? A whale or a shoe?
My snorkel's stuck, it's quite the view!
Fish make faces, they swim on by,
I wave my arms, but I'm not a guy!

A treasure chest, but it's just some junk,
A pirate's hat, what a smelly funk!
I'm diving deep with laughter loud,
In this wondrous scene, I'm quite the crowd!

Secrets of the Surf

Bubbles rise, fish wear shades,
Starfish dancing in cool cascades.
Seagulls squawk, they're quite the show,
Surfboards float, they steal the flow.

Jellyfish float, like bobbing balloons,
Seaweed wigs, they change their tunes.
Crabs breakdance upon the sand,
While dolphins trade jokes, oh so grand!

Frogs in trunks, hopping in glee,
Sandy feet, a beach jubilee.
Octopus leads a conga line,
Under the sun, everything's fine.

With waves that cackle, and tides that tease,
Mermaids laugh under the palm trees.
So come, join in this silly spree,
Where every splash is pure jubilee!

Aquatic Reverie

The fish wear ties, quite debonair,
Whales tell tales with a splash of flair.
Crabs play poker on the shore,
While squids attempt to juggle more.

Seahorses parade in tiny cars,
Starfish gaze at bright, twinkling stars.
Turtles surf on pastel waves,
Waving to shells, they're such brave knaves.

Seagulls break out in song and dance,
While jellyfish dream in a goofy trance.
Dolphins flip with a twist of grace,
Wishing for cake in this ocean space.

So let's frolic where the waters gleam,
In a world that's sillier than a dream.
With every splash, let laughter ring,
Embrace the joy that the sea can bring!

Lullaby of the Tides

In the shallow, bubbles pop,
Clams play tic-tac-toe non-stop.
Under the waves, they giggle and sing,
Where every splash feels like spring.

Fish in bow ties hold a debate,
While sea cucumbers can't be late.
Sandcastles guarded by crabs so bold,
Building their kingdoms, watched with gold.

The seaweed sways, a groovy dance,
Coral reefs in a bright romance.
Octopus knitters have yarn to spare,
Creating hats for fish with flair.

So as the tides rock you to sleep,
Dream of the laughter, the joy to keep.
Dive into waves of fun and delight,
With the lullaby of stars at night!

Shoreline Whispers

Seagulls gossip on the breeze,
While clams share tales with the seaweeds.
Sand dollars giggle as they lie,
Building castles as waves pass by.

Crabs in capes march down the shore,
Wandering warriors with hearts of roar.
Nudibranchs strut in rainbow hues,
While fish don sunglasses and surf their cruise.

Mermaid meetings at dusk, so spry,
Planning the next great ocean fry.
With laughter bubbly – a tidal wave,
In a world where every creature's brave.

So listen close to the sea's delight,
Where laughter cascades like stars at night.
Join the fun as the sun dips low,
In the whispers of waves where wonders flow!

Whispers of the Tides

Crabs wearing hats dance in a line,
Turtles hula-hooping, looking quite fine.
Jellyfish jelly, a wobbly treat,
Octopus juggling, with eight arms to greet.

Seashells gossip, they gossip all day,
Starfish playing cards, oh what a display!
Dolphins are laughing, splashing nearby,
While seagulls are singing, oh me, oh my!

Blue Horizons Beckon

Fish in bowties swim with such flair,
Seahorses strumming on banjos with care.
Coconuts falling from palm trees so high,
Pufferfish puffing, oh my, oh my!

Corals are painting, with colors so bright,
Anemones having a tickle-fight night.
Under the sun, they're planning a show,
Who knew the sea had such a fun flow?

Sailors of the Dreaming Sea

Pirates in pajamas sail out with glee,
Mermaids with sunglasses sip tea by the sea.
A treasure of jellybeans, sought by a crab,
Finding their fortune, with giggles, they grab.

Whales wearing scarves sing songs from the deep,
While pufferfish giggle and bubble their sleep.
With laughter and joy, the waves do agree,
Life's just a circus on this wavy spree!

Beneath the Aquamarine Canvas

Clownfish painting each other's bright cheeks,
Seals doing somersaults, look at those tweaks!
Waves play tag with the rocks on the shore,
While crabs in a conga line dance evermore.

Bubbles are bouncing, in colors so wild,
Frogs on the beach are jumping like a child.
The seaweed sways, like it's part of the act,
Where laughter and whimsy gets tangled, in fact!

Gateway to Wonders

A fish with a hat swam by,
Sipping juice, oh my, oh my!
He winked with a playful fin,
"Join this party, dive on in!"

A crab learned to do the jig,
He twirled with a scoot and a wig.
The octopus clapped with glee,
"Dance like you're wild and free!"

A turtle in shades took a stroll,
With a beach ball, he felt whole.
He laughed each step down the sand,
"Welcome, folks, to this grand land!"

Seashells giggled under the sun,
Joking about races for fun.
And all the waves joined the cheer,
"Let's celebrate all year!"

Awash in Blue

A dolphin told jokes with a splish,
The crowd clapped, "What's your wish?"
He leaped high and dashed down low,
"More puns, and let the fun flow!"

A seal had a talent to sing,
But forgot all the words of spring.
Instead, he hummed to his friends,
"Please excuse, this never ends!"

Jellyfish wiggled side by side,
In a dance that they couldn't hide.
They tripped over coral and laughed,
"No need for perfection, just a craft!"

The seabirds cawed with a cheer,
"Come and join us, never fear!"
As laughter echoed through the tide,
A perfect playground far and wide!

Cradle of the Waves

In a cove, a jelly named Lou,
Made a hat from seaweed, who knew?
He said, "Fashion's the name of the game,
Top of the tides, I'll find my fame!"

A starfish tried to breakdance right,
But ended up stuck, oh, what a sight!
A sea turtle gave a gentle shove,
"Don't you worry, it's all out of love!"

Two mackerels raced in a rush,
One slipped and made the sand flush.
Giggling fish all gathered 'round,
"Let's crown the silliest in town!"

As the waves rolled with chortles and cheers,
The sea clowns performed, conquering fears.
All creatures joined in merriment bright,
In this cradle, pure delight!

Ocean Breeze

A seagull tried on a pair of shades,
Said, "I'm cool in these ocean glades!"
He strutted with flair, wings out wide,
"Just call me the beach-side guide!"

A crab in a truck made of sand,
Drove past with tickets all in hand.
"Come see the show, it's great fun!
I promise it's much more than a pun!"

Waves giggled and splashed on the shore,
"Let's have a contest; who can roar?"
The best sound came from an old walrus,
"Check this out, I just can't fuss!"

As the twilight painted the sky,
A party of creatures danced nearby.
With laughter and joy, they sang and played,
Forever young in this fun parade!

Secrets of the Blue

Fish in tuxedos swim with glee,
Starfish are dancing, just wait and see.
Crabs do the cha-cha on the beach,
While mermaids just giggle, out of reach.

Octopuses juggle, oh what a sight,
Seagulls wear sunglasses, feeling just right.
The seaweed throws parties, full of green,
While dolphins play tag, sleek and lean.

Turtles on surfboards, catching the waves,
Blowfish tell jokes, oh how it saves.
Every shell holds a secret so grand,
In this watery world, life is unplanned.

Even the plankton join in the fun,
Doing the limbo, everyone's spun.
Under the sun, everything's bright,
In this wacky kingdom, pure delight!

Coastal Reverie

Bubbles rise up like tiny balloons,
Crabs with binoculars, studying moons.
Seashells gossip as tides drift away,
Laughing at tourists who don't know to stay.

Jellyfish jelly, they spread on the sand,
Seagulls trading secrets that are oh so bland.
Starfish play poker with a wink and a grin,
In their own underwater version of sin.

Squids with a splash paint the ocean bright,
While clams hold a concert, what a lovely sight!
Wave after wave, they sway with a beat,
As fish form a chorus, tapping their feet.

A finned cabaret, a vibrant affair,
With laughter and bubbles hanging in the air.
No need for a map in this jubilant show,
Just let yourself go, let your laughter flow!

Serene Shores

The crabs roll in, looking for snacks,
While the sea turtles take lazy laps.
Flip-flops and laughter dance on the breeze,
As the ocean whispers its cheeky teas.

Clams in their shells read magazines,
While dolphins polish their shiny routines.
Seagulls shoplift fries from picnic spreads,
Sandy-footed kids run, feeling well-fed.

Cocktails served in coconut shells,
Freestyle mermaids conjuring spells.
As the sun sets, the bubbles lift high,
Laughter wraps around like clouds in the sky.

Fishes that giggle, a humorous sight,
The sea foam chuckles, exploding with light.
Join in the fun, come frolic and play,
In this calm little corner, where silliness stays!

Poetry of the Deep

In the dark depths, shrimp throw a rave,
Anemones wear party hats, oh how they wave.
Worms in tuxedos bob like they're sassy,
While clams take selfies, looking all classy.

Seahorses twirl with the utmost finesse,
As eels tell tales, causing a mess.
In coral caverns, the laughter is bright,
The fish rescue jokes just out of sight.

Drifting with jelly, all gooey and real,
Pufferfish puff up, but it's all just a deal.
Sharks tell ghost stories, tickling a spine,
While whales serenade with a hiccuping line.

So join in the depths, where mischief is king,
With bubbles and giggles, hear the ocean sing.
A world full of whimsy, so easy to find,
In the vibrant abyss, leave your worries behind!

Tides of Tranquility

Waves crash like laughter, oh so loud,
Seagulls steal fries from the beachgoer's crowd.
A crab wearing sunglasses wobbles by,
While jellyfish dance, oh me, oh my!

Sandcastles sway like they're in a ball,
The tide comes in, and they take a fall.
Buckets and shovels tossed aside,
As kids chase a breeze, giggling with pride.

The sun's so bright, it sings on my skin,
Laughter spills over like it's a win.
Flip-flops flapping in sync with the beat,
And the ocean waves mingle with my feet!

A dolphin leaps out for a peek,
Messy ice cream drips down my cheek.
With each splash, a bubble of cheer,
In this sandy wonderland, there's nothing to fear!

Coral Dreams

Underwater disco, the fish in a twist,
They flop and they flounder, who could resist?
A clownfish with jokes, oh what a sight,
Making friends with a shrimp, dancing all night.

Coral castles hiding treasures so bright,
Each nook has a story, a quirky delight.
Octopus jugglers show off their style,
As starfish sit back, relaxing awhile.

The sea turtles race, but they're slow as can be,
Hinting that winning isn't the key.
With bubbles of laughter up into the blue,
We laugh and we twirl; come join in, won't you?

Pearls of wisdom in fishy chat rooms,
Sea urchins gossip while sharing their blooms.
In this underwater tale, we smile and play,
With fins and with fins, we'll drift the day away!

Seaside Symphony

The waves play a tune, a rhythm divine,
Seashells clap hands, they join in the line.
Sandy drummers bang on buckets with glee,
While beach balls bounce to the symphony!

A crab on a stage, with a tiny blue hat,
Bouncing around like a zany acrobat.
Seagulls join in, they squawk and they dive,
This seaside concert really comes alive!

The sun dips low, painting skies with gold,
A sunset encore, a sight to behold.
With laughter and song, the day winds down,
And fish in the sea wear their crowns like a crown.

As night falls gently, the stars start to gleam,
We pack up our laughter and drift off to dream.
With waves as our lullaby, soft and sweet,
In this seaside symphony, life feels complete!

Moonlit Shores

The moon prances out with a silvery smile,
While crabs do the cha-cha along the mile.
Starfish in tuxedos, oh what a sight,
They twirl and they spin under soft moonlight.

The sand's like a dance floor, oh so fine,
With footprints of laughter and a neat wine.
Every wave that comes has a funny intent,
Tickling our toes, it's a full-on event.

The jellyfish float like balloons in the dark,
Flashing their colors, each one a spark.
But watch out for seaweed, it's sneaky, I swear,
It wraps around ankles, a slippery snare!

As night drifts along, and stars take their cue,
Crabs play the drums, and dolphins break through.
With giggles and splashes, the night waves goodbye,
In this moonlit paradise, we all laugh and fly!

Tranquil Splash

A fish in a tuxedo, quite a sight,
Dances with dolphins, what a delight!
Crabs with their pinchers, playing tag,
While seagulls squawk, looking for a brag.

Turtles in sunglasses, chill on the sand,
Building sandcastles, oh so grand.
Starfish gossiping, oh what a scene,
While jellyfish float like a wobbly queen.

A picnic of seaweed, tastes a bit green,
But clams crack jokes like you've never seen.
A dolphin made a tweet; it went quite viral,
While sea cucumbers wish for a trial.

So here on the shore, laughter does swell,
With creatures who share their strange tales to tell.
Where the waves keep rolling, and smiles abound,
In this whimsical world, joy can be found.

Maritime Muse

A whale in a hat, he sings quite loud,
While crabs in the corner form a conga crowd.
Octopuses juggle, such clever displays,
And fish hold a contest for best jokes in rays.

Gulls wear sunglasses, oh what a sight,
Stealing popcorn, they fly left and right.
A clam in a flip-flop, feels quite grand,
While sea urchins cheer for their rock band.

A crab with a mustache, full of wise cracks,
Tells tales of the shrimp who's got quite the knack.
The seaweed schools dance in a synchronized show,
Making a splash, their giggles in tow.

And as the sun sets on this salty spree,
We'll dance with the tide, forever carefree.
With laughs that echo through bubbles and foam,
In this quirky kingdom, we've found our home.

Coastline Chronicles

Pelicans plop, in a silly way,
Waddling along in the sun's bright ray.
Starfish on stilts think they're so cool,
While splashing sea otters make a splash pool.

The crabs throw a party, oh what a bash,
Dancing on rocks, like a wild, fun crash.
Seagulls in disco, with feathers a-flare,
While lobsters compete for the best pair.

Shells tell their stories with giggles and grins,
Playing hide-and-seek, where everyone wins.
The shrimp host a talent show, no time to nap,
As a clam in a bowtie gives a big clap.

With seafoam on toes, we laugh and we play,
In this minuscule realm, where dreams float away.
Every wave brings laughter, a joyful reprieve,
In our quirky beach life, there's nothing to leave.

Beneath the Celestial

Anemones dance under the moon's gentle glow,
Mermaids with ukuleles put on quite a show.
A pufferfish giggles, puffed up with glee,
While seahorses challenge each other to flee.

Dolphins on skates play tag with the stars,
As narwhals craft jokes about fixing their cars.
A jellyfish waltzes, in a gown made of light,
While krill tap their feet, oh what a sight!

The sand crabs are busy, on a quest for their snack,
While schools of bright fish form a conga, in fact.
With laughter erupting like bubbles in tide,
Spreading joy all around, can't let it subside.

When the moon takes a bow and the sun starts to beam,
We'll tumble in waves, lost in laughter's dream.
Celebrating the night with a giggle and splash,
In this whimsical world, where silly hopes clash.

Serenade of Salt and Sun

The seagulls squawk, oh what a show,
They steal my fries, how low can they go?
With sandy toes and sunscreen smeared,
I'm pretty sure my beach outfit's weird!

A crab in shades, sunbathing wide,
He's got more style than I ever tried.
As waves go splat, I jump with glee,
But my ice cream's now a sea creature's spree!

With surfboards stacked like toasty bread,
My buddy wipes out and lands on his head.
We laugh and splash, forgetting the fuss,
Life's simple here, no need to rush!

So here I sit on my sandy throne,
With prancing dolphins as my own.
Let's raise a toast with fruit drinks in hand,
In this goofy wonderland, oh so grand!

Secrets of the Deep Blue

Beneath the waves, the fish wear ties,
Throwing a party, oh what a surprise!
Octopus dancing, no shoes on his feet,
With jellyfish wobbles, quite the feast!

The turtles are slow but full of charm,
Offering hugs, just don't sound the alarm!
A dolphin breaks in with a flip and a spin,
Who knew being silly was a way to win?

The seashells gossip, they chatter away,
"Look at that starfish, he's styling today!"
With kelp as confetti, the fun's not quite done,
We're all here together, laughing in the sun!

So dive right down, don't be shy or meek,
In this busy blue world, everyone's chic!
The secrets abound in this watery sprawl,
Let's celebrate together – our joyful brawl!

Waves of Enchanted Shores

At the water's edge, our dreams take flight,
We sprint from the waves in sheer delight.
A seaweed crown, so regal and green,
Not quite the fashion I had in mind for my scene!

As sandcastles rise and then plummet with glee,
A flock of ducks holds a comedy spree.
They waddle and quack, making quite a fuss,
While we try to escape – a wet, sandy bus!

The tide teases us, it pulls with a grin,
"Come join my dance, let the fun begin!"
We slip and we slide, with giggles galore,
What's better than laughter by the shore?

So toss in a belly flop or a splash,
Make friends with a crab that will dance in a flash!
With sunsets that shimmer and skies painted gold,
Every wave's a treasure, waiting to be told.

The Siren's Call

They sing sweet songs, those mermaids fair,
But don't be fooled, they're up for a dare!
With glittery tails and a wink so sly,
They'll lure you in and then make you pie!

A fish is doing the cha-cha with flair,
While crabs collect seashells like they're rare.
"Join us!" they shout, "For giggles and fun,
We've got a treasure hunt under the sun!"

Bubbles laugh as they float all around,
Making silly shapes that spin on the ground.
Octopus juggles with shells all a-dazzle,
While the clams crack jokes just to raise a frazzle!

So heed the call of the sea and the breeze,
Join in the frolic, soak up the tease.
Life's too short for seriousness, you see,
In this splashy realm, you're as wild as the sea!

Voyage of Shells and Stars

On a sandy beach, shells clash and cheer,
The crabs are playing games, oh dear!
Seagulls squawk while doing their dance,
They steal my snacks, not leaving a chance.

Starfish scatter like they're on a spree,
They laugh at my footprints, "Look at me!"
This driftwood's a ship, I'm a captain bold,
But it seems my crew is just a pile of gold!

The waves make faces as they roll in,
They tickle my toes; oh, what a win!
Every splash brings giggles, it seems,
As I float along, lost in my dreams.

So here's to laughter under the sun's rays,
In this silly world, we spend our days.
The shells on the shore, they're all quite witty,
In this sea of joy, nothing's too gritty!

Embrace of the Endless Blue

Bubbles bubble up in a bubbly row,
Fish play hide-and-seek, putting on a show.
A whale waves hello with a splash and a grin,
While jellyfish giggle as I float in.

Octopus chefs whip up a feast,
Mussels squeak jokes, they're quite the beast.
Underwater comedy, what a blast,
With sea cucumbers, I'll never be last!

The dolphins make flips, and I can't compete,
But wait, is that seaweed tangled on my feet?
With every splash, I'm losing my grace,
This salty tango turns into a race!

Yet amidst the fun and the aquatic games,
The fish call my name, it's all quite the fame.
With a wink and a wave, they bid me adieu,
In this jolly blue world, there's plenty to do!

Dance of the Water Spirits

In the gentle sway, the waves start to prance,
The mermaids are giggling, joining the dance.
Shells are their partners, all shiny and bright,
While seaweed twirls in the shimmering light.

"Come join our party!" the fish all declare,
But I flounder around, tangled in hair.
A sea star sticks out its tongue with a grin,
As I shoot for the surface, let's not let them win!

Coral formations are tapping their feet,
While crabs in tuxedos get up to the beat.
Anemones sway, they know how to groove,
In the wavy dance floor, we all try to move!

So twirl with the tides, don't be shy or coy,
In this splashing, laughing, aquatic joy.
With a splash and a laugh, the night carries on,
As I wade through the waves till the dancing is gone!

Tidepool Treasures

In a puddle of joy, look what I find,
A crab in a bowtie, so very refined!
A sea anemone, waving like a flag,
"Step right up!" it beckons, "Join in the brag!"

Tiny fish giggles, they swim all about,
With snails on the sidelines, they cheer and shout.
A starfish is juggling, oh what a sight,
"In this little world, we have all the light!"

The seashells are chattering, laying their claim,
"What's that in your pocket? A sand dollar fame?"
I laugh and I ponder, so happy and bold,
In this magical world, treasures unfold.

So let's play in the tidepools and splash with delight,
With creatures like us, the joy feels so right.
In this watery wonder, laughter is free,
In the pocket of a tidepool, come dance with me!

Fluid Reverie

Waves dance with a silly sway,
Seagulls squawk in a comical way.
Fish wear sunglasses, quite the show,
While dolphins glide and put on a glow.

Buckets of laughter spill all around,
Crabs do the cha-cha on the wet ground.
Jellyfish jiggle, oh what a sight,
As beach balls bounce with sheer delight.

Sandcastles crumble with giggles and glee,
A sandman waves, as happy as can be.
Children chase waves, their shouts fill the air,
A symphony of fun, without a care.

The tide rolls in, a slippery beast,
As everyone runs, it's a water-filled feast.
Splashing and laughing, we shout with pride,
In this fluid world where joys collide.

Vista of the Aqua

Salty air tickles our noses,
Mermaids giggle as the tide dozes.
Octopuses juggle starfish with flair,
While sea turtles race without a care.

Fluffy clouds drift, like cotton candy,
Waves play tag, they're feeling dandy.
Squirrels don swimsuits; what a sight!
As seashells gossip about that night.

A crab with shades sings a jolly tune,
Under the watch of a snoozing moon.
Tidal pools bubble like a cheerful stew,
And all of our worries just float away too.

We build our dreams in castles of sand,
With ice cream cones clasped in each hand.
Laughter echoes as splashes ignite,
In this magical vista, everything's right.

Retreat of the Tides

Waves peek out, then back they retreat,
Leaving behind a treasure hunt fleet.
Barnacles wear hats, looking so grand,
As seashells play dress-up on the soft sand.

Gulls with sunglasses stroll with such flair,
While beach umbrellas wave in the air.
Flip-flops fly, oh what a sight!
As salty breeze dances in delight.

Seasick sea cucumbers sway with cheer,
Whales do the worm when they come near.
Sprinklers go wild, all join the fun,
In this playful retreat under the sun.

Crabs in their mittens challenge the breeze,
Splashing and laughing, doing as they please.
Under the sun, we giggle and glide,
In this whimsical world of the changing tide.

Footprints in the Sand

Tiny feet tread lightly on golden shores,
Leaving behind stories, and giggling roars.
The sun winks down, a partner in crime,
While seagulls squawk at the silliest rhyme.

Footprints lead to where laughter begins,
As waves crash in, wearing silly grins.
Starfish hold court, quite proud of their shape,
As beach balls bounce, and a crab takes a break.

Kites soar high, tickling the clouds,
While everyone chases their laughter aloud.
Sandals abandoned, kids dance around,
With joy left in footprints cast on the ground.

The tide rolls in, washing away what's left,
But memories cling on, so utterly cleft.
In this fantastical land of warmth and sun,
We find that the fun has only begun.

Embracing the Abyss

Bubbles up like a mermaid's laugh,
Octopus in a snazzy scarf.
Turtles race with the speed of snails,
While jellyfish tell silly tales.

Fish in suits swim by in style,
Winking at seagulls, oh what a smile!
Sandcastles whine when the tide rolls in,
'Why do you always have to win?'

Crabs are dancing with funky moves,
Clams holding hands in their own grooves.
Starfish argue whose turn it is,
In this game of shellfish biz!

A whale cracked a joke, it made us groan,
With a splash, it swam off alone.
In this watery world, we laugh with glee,
Even plankton have a sense of spree.

Dance of the Seafoam

Seafoam bubbles like a ticklish giggle,
Dancing waves do a wiggly wiggle.
Seashells gossip in whispers loud,
As the sand grins beneath the crowd.

Crabby critters have a conga line,
While dolphins dive like they're fine wine.
Seagulls squawk with a flair for drama,
Arguing 'bout who's the best karma.

Flounder flaunts with a flip and a spin,
While seaweed sways, oh what a grin!
Starfish take selfies, who needs a phone?
'Look at our tan!' they happily moan.

As the tide rolls out, they wave goodbye,
While sea cucumbers let out a sigh.
They'll be back for the next big show,
In this frothy dance, it's all about flow.

Horizon's Embrace

The sun sets down, a tangerine cheer,
A crab in shades says, 'I'm over here!'
Seagulls prank with their high-pitched calls,
As wavelets giggle and gently fall.

Mermaids swap tales of the latest scoop,
While fiddler crabs hold a tiny troupe.
With fins that jive, they glide and sway,
In a world where nonsense rules the day.

The turtles debate the best pizza treat,
'Anchovy's great,' says one with a beat.
Clams crack up at the jelly's dance,
Who knew the deep had such good romance?

A starfish throws a party on the reef,
While everyone pops in without a chief.
In this realm of silly, joy's in the chase,
Getting lost in laughter is the heart of this place.

Sea Glass Memories

Shiny shards of a bright past gleam,
Like fish who dream a silly dream.
Waves toss stories from long ago,
Riding bubbles in a frothy show.

Old flip-flops float as boats on the tide,
While a washed-up anchor starts to glide.
'What's my job?' it ponders with glee,
'Finding treasure or lost jubilee?'

The gulls make memes of the sun-kissed sand,
As crabs perform with a nightly band.
They snap their claws to the ocean beat,
Even barnacles tap their tiny feet!

In this realm of forgotten flair,
Every bubble holds a secret to share.
So gather the laughter, the quirks and sass,
In the depths of the sea, we've got class!

Jewel of the Deep

A fish in a tux, oh what a sight,
Swirling and twirling, in pure delight.
He stole a pearl from a sleepy clam,
Now he's a star, a real big slam!

Octopus on roller skates, quite the feat,
He slips and he slides, can't find his seat.
With eight arms waving in wild surprise,
He trips over seashells, oh how he cries!

A crab with a crown, in his royal pose,
Strutting like royalty, striking a pose.
But underneath that shell, so grand and bright,
His royal throne is just a pile of fright!

As jellyfish float like balloons on a spree,
They giggle and wiggle, oh can't you see?
In this underwater ball of silly cheer,
It's the best kind of bash, bring all your peers!

Rhythm of the Reef

The sea turtles groove in a slow, cool dance,
With flippers flapping, they've got a chance.
A dolphin with shades, oh he's really fly,
Singing sea shanties as he jumps high!

Clownfish play tricks, oh what a scene,
In an anemone, they're the fishy queens.
They throw a splash party in bubbly glee,
It's splashes and bubbles, just let it be!

Starfish with drumsticks, tapping away,
Creating beats that make the sea sway.
While the seahorse strums on a coral guitar,
Their tunes take us far, oh yes, they're a star!

Navigating the currents, that's how they roll,
Underwater parties, that's their main goal!
With each wave a joke, laughter abounds,
In the rhythm of the reef, joy knows no bounds!

Sailing into Bliss

A pirate with a parrot sings off-key,
While steering a ship made of jelly and tea.
With a treasure map drawn on a pizza slice,
Every wave's a giggle, oh isn't it nice?

Coconuts dance as the captain shouts,
"Yarr matey, let's see what the wind's about!"
But sail they shall, with a squawk and a cheer,
Their booty awaits, right over there!

Along came a crab wearing a captain's hat,
He stole the show, just like that!
With a wink and a wave, off he did trot,
Now he's the leader of this motley lot!

As stars shine bright in a jellyfish glow,
They sail through the night, moving slow.
In seas of laughter, where silliness reigns,
This voyage is wild, oh what fun it gains!

Tidal Tranquility

At dawn, a whale hums a lullaby,
To sleepy sea gulls flitting by.
A starfish snores on a tranquil bed,
While clams dream dreams of buttered bread.

Seahorses sip tea in a coral café,
Giggling and gossiping all day.
With tales of swashbucklers and treasures untold,
The ocean's a stage for comedy, bold!

As the waves bubble up with a tickle and tease,
Anemones laugh in the soft, salty breeze.
A mermaid with hair made of seaweed and shells,
Cracks jokes that ring like enchanting bells!

With antics and pranks that float all around,
In the calm of the tides, joy knows no bound.
So let's all dive in, and join the fun spree,
In this tide of laughter, let your heart be free!

Sands of Time

With flip-flops on, I run so fast,
But the sand sticks tight, what a blast!
I trip and fall, a comical sight,
A crab scuttles by, laughing in delight.

Buckets in hand, we build a grand dome,
But seagulls dive in, saying, "This is my home!"
Sandcastles collapse, to my utter despair,
While kids cheer and throw sand everywhere!

A sunburned nose, I try to look cool,
Trying to surf with a board that's a stool!
I wipe out again, much to their glee,
The ocean's giggles are too much for me.

When seashells sing and dolphins dance,
We laugh in fits, seized by chance.
I say I'm pro as I sip my drink,
But floundering fish give me time to think.

Celestial Waveforms

The stars above mirror the waves below,
While I attempt to surf, much to my woe!
Splashing in foam, a water ballet,
But I just look like I'm drowning in play.

A jellyfish floats by, oh what a prank,
I wave at it, but it's just an old plank.
"Friendly fish" I call, but they swim away,
Guess I'm not the catch of the day!

The moon winks down with a silvery grin,
As I chase my hat that the wind stole so thin.
Round and round like a dizzying shell,
I think I'll just sit, in this watery swell.

Comets zoom across the night's sly smile,
I build a sand fort, but it's not worth the while.
With grains in my pants and laughter loud,
I'm the quirky one amongst the crowd.

Beyond the Breakers

I peek beyond the foamy crest,
A dolphin decides to put me to the test!
He leaps and spins, oh what a sight,
While I attempt to catch some light.

Board in hand, I'm ready to glide,
But the wave swallows me instead of my pride.
I pop up gasping, water in my nose,
A seal nearby gives me a pose!

Sun-kissed and salty, with plans so grand,
I dig for treasure in shifting sand.
But what do I find? Just a rubber shoe,
The world's greatest pirate, it seems, is a goof too!

As sun sets low, I watch the scene,
My friends giggle harder than I have ever seen.
It's a battle of wit, with waves as our foes,
In the salty air, joy freely flows.

Currents of Calm

Under the shade, with drinks piled high,
Laughter floats in as the seagulls fly.
I sip my coconut, pretending to sway,
But a wave crashes down, ruining my day!

The sand is so warm, I dig like a kid,
Playing in castles, oh how I hid!
But the tide comes in, my fortress is lost,
I scream and shout, "What a heavy cost!"

I dance salsa with waves lapping at my toes,
While trying to avoid that sneaky hose.
My friends just laugh as I gallivant around,
Sandy and silly, pure joy we found!

In the twilight glow, as stars start to gleam,
We gather our treasures, share every dream.
With smiles wide and stories to trade,
The night whispers secrets the ocean has made.

Aurora Above the Rippled Horizon

Fish in funny hats dance,
Underneath the moon's glance,
Jellybeans float by for fun,
Sandy toes, oh what a run!

Crabs wear sunglasses, what a sight,
Taking sunbaths, feeling light,
Seashells gossip, tales unfold,
Treasures found, oh so bold!

Waves tickle feet, laughter rings,
Starfish throw their bling-bling things,
Octopuses juggle, what a spree,
Life's a joke in salty glee!

Mermaids giggle, swaying hair,
Paddleboards drifting without a care,
In this splashy world, hooray!
Come join the frolic, let's play all day!

Where the Seagulls Soar

Seagulls wearing tiny shoes,
Sing and dance, they love to cruise,
Sandcastles tumble in delight,
As crabs cheer from left to right.

Kites are flying, swoosh and swirl,
A beach ball bounces, give it a whirl,
Flip-flops flapping, what a scene,
Under the sun with ocean's sheen.

Wave a hello to a bright blue whale,
Whispering secrets in a fishy tale,
Laughter echoes, splashes abound,
Life's a party, joy is found!

As the tide rolls, laughter grows,
Dodging surprises from ocean flows,
Seagulls squawking their humorous tunes,
A sunny day, with silly boons!

Kaleidoscopic Dreams of the Wave

Rainbow fish wear polka spots,
Wiggling in their dancing knots,
Crazy currents twist and twirl,
A splashy party to unfurl.

Barnacles play peek-a-boo,
While dolphins put on a show for two,
Flip-flops floating, laughter beams,
Life's a circus in sandy dreams!

Mermaids munch on pop-corn treats,
As turtles groove to funky beats,
Shells are clapping, here's the plan,
Join the fun, caught in the jam!

With every wave, a chuckle flies,
Underneath the big blue skies,
Seaweed wiggles, all in glee,
Join the dance, just you and me!

Anemones in the Twilight

Anemones bounce in the twilight glow,
Tickling fish in their colorful show,
Starry-eyed seahorses spin around,
Their laughter echoes, a joyful sound.

Glowfish flash with silly grace,
A dance-off starts, an epic race,
Shrimp with shades, boogie on sand,
Life's a party, just as planned!

Nudibranchs strut in their finest threads,
While sea cucumbers play with their heads,
Coral castles filled with cheer,
A whimsical realm, come on, my dear!

As the sun dips below the waves,
Life sparkles with giggles and raves,
Join the fun where friendships flow,
In this bubbly world, let's steal the show!

Siren's Call

Upon the rocks, she sings so sweet,
With seaweed hair and fishy feet.
'Come dance with me beneath the waves!'
I swear, she can't be one of the knaves!

Her voice is like a rubber duck,
It quacks and echoes, oh what luck!
But when I swim, she pulls me down,
Now I'm the laughingstock in town!

School of fish with shades on tight,
They point and giggle at my plight.
I try to look cool in the deep,
But all I do is blub and weep!

So heed this tale next time you roam,
Beware the sirens in their foam.
For while their charm may seem so neat,
They'll have you tripping on your feet!

Island Serenity

Under palm trees, drinks in hand,
A coconut fell, oh what a stand!
It bounced and rolled, then knocked me down,
The picnic turned into a clown town!

The hammock swayed, a perfect sight,
But how I swung and missed the height!
With every twist, a laugh did swell,
I landed face-first in a shell!

The crabs at sunset held a feast,
I joined them, thinking I'm the beast.
They scuttled off, and left me stuck,
That was my luck, that was my luck!

So revel in this blissful fun,
With every blunder, there's a pun.
For on this island filled with glee,
Laughter's the best drink, don't you see?

Depths of Delight

In waters blue, I dove with grace,
Chased a fish, but lost my place.
Now I'm tangled in seaweed hair,
With bubbles rising from despair!

The octopus laughed, what a sight,
As I flailed and fought with all my might.
He waved his tentacles like a flag,
I shook my head and felt the drag!

A dolphin leaped with great delight,
He offered me a ride, what a fright!
But as I clung on for dear life,
He spun me 'round—oh, what a strife!

So in these depths of mirth and play,
Remember, splashing's not the way.
For laughter echoes 'neath the sea,
And trust me, it's much better free!

Azure Allure

The sky is blue, the sea is bright,
I thought I'd swim to my delight.
But the seagulls swooped and stole my snacks,
Now I'm left with just the cracks!

I spotted a treasure chest with glee,
But when it opened, oh me, oh my!
Out popped a lobster in full dance,
He taught me moves, a crazy chance!

Shells were clapping, fish join the beat,
I found my flippers, oh what a feat!
But slipped on kelp, I spun around,
Now I'm the star of this underwater crown!

So if you venture to waves so blue,
Prepare for giggles, and laughter too.
For in this world of salty flares,
Life is best when it's full of tears!

Nautical Dreams

Sailing on a shoe, what a sight,
Fish sing songs, oh what a night!
Seagulls tell tales of lost socks,
While octopuses dance in frocks.

Crabs throw parties in the sand,
They've got a DJ, oh so grand!
Turtles breakdance, what a view,
Everyone's laughing, who knew?

Sharks wear hats, they think they're cool,
While dolphins splash in our own pool.
Anchors aweigh for ships of dreams,
Life's a joke, or so it seems!

Mermaids gossip, it's quite the show,
Who's got the best seashells, do you know?
What a life under waves so fine,
Playing chess with shrimp, oh divine!

Shores of Solitude

I found a crab on the lonely shore,
He tried to dance, fell, oh what a roar!
Seashells whispered, 'Come join the fun!'
While starfish giggled in the sun.

A beach ball floated, but ran away,
Cooperative waves, wouldn't stay!
Seagulls squawked, 'That's not a cat!'
While I just pondered, 'What's up with that?'

The sand was hot, the sun was bright,
Fell asleep on the beach one night.
Woke up confused, a crab in my shoe,
"How do you do?" he seemed to coo.

A dolphin jumped with a sneaky grin,
"Want to play? Just don't let me win!"
Laughter echoes through this space,
The shores of solitude, a joyful place!

Colors of a Sunset Sea

The sunset painted the sky so pink,
While jellyfish danced, they made me think.
Fish had a party, they invited me,
Their music was weird, but so very free.

Octopus wore a tie, quite posh,
While crabs debated, 'Which way to wash?'
Seashells clinked, a curious band,
Making music all across the sand.

As the waves rolled in, I took a dive,
Caught a bubble, felt so alive!
Mermaids laughed, "Oh look, it's a guy,
Join the fun or just say bye!"

The colors faded, the night was near,
Fish in tuxedos, oh, what a cheer!
As I closed my eyes, hope to see,
Those silly creatures swim back to me.

Gentle Currents

A current pulled my hat away,
I chased it down, 'What a silly play!'
Fish giggled hard, as I did race,
But all my flailing left no trace.

A turtle offered me some tea,
Said, "Take it slow, come swim with me!"
We toasted to the jellybeans,
Making wishes on our dreams.

Seashells whispered secrets so grand,
Said, "Watch out for the beachball band!"
I tripped and fell, made quite a splash,
While dolphins laughed, oh what a crash!

The gentle waves sang a sweet tune,
Under the watch of the big, bright moon.
So here's to currents that make us smile,
Let's ride the waves and stay awhile!

Pulse of the Planet

Bubbles float like tiny boats,
Fish wear hats, and they take notes.
Seagulls squawk with goofy glee,
Sandy toes and crabby tea.

Jellyfish dance, a wobbly show,
Octopus in a chef's white fro.
Coral reefs wear party hats,
And dolphins chat with polite spats.

Starfish doing the latest jig,
Clams conga, their shells they dig.
A beach ball bounces, oh what fun!
Everyone swims till the day is done.

Seashells giggle on the shore,
As waves tell jokes that we adore.
Underwater, the laughter flows,
Who knew tides could strike such poses?

Glistening Horizons

Mermaids playing leapfrog near,
Shiny scales, they wink and cheer.
Crabs in sunglasses stroll around,
They're quite the stylish fools we've found.

Seaweed sways, a funky dance,
While plankton glow, they take a chance.
A whale is painting with his tail,
Creating art that'll never fail.

Surfboards giggle, catching waves,
While sea turtles climb on knaves.
The horizon sparkles with delight,
As starfish wish for pizza night.

Windy whispers fill the air,
With silly jokes and beachy flair.
The sun dips down, all aglow,
In this land where laughs just flow.

Wistful Waters

Puddles hold a playful grin,
Splashing laughter found within.
Seashells whisper secret dreams,
In breezy winds, they burst at seams.

Lighthouse beams do funny dance,
While crabs break into a prance.
Floaty ducks with silly hats,
Join in with the chatty cats.

Waterfalls have giggly coughs,
As frogs do flips from moss to troughs.
The waves splash jokes with every crest,
Making sure we're ever blessed.

But as the darkness starts to sway,
Starfish wish on whales at play.
They twinkle dreams from dusk to dawn,
In waters where the laughter's drawn.

Cascading Crystals

Raindrops dance on ocean's skin,
With every splash, a cheeky grin.
Glistening gems of sunlit cheer,
Make fishy friends shed their fear.

Bubble parties pop and whirl,
As mermaids teach the sea to twirl.
A crab sidesteps, trying to tease,
While sea cucumbers roll with ease.

Laughing waves and splashes bright,
Tickle toes with sheer delight.
Turtles wear their finest flair,
Strutting like they just don't care.

In this place where fun's the goal,
Every creature finds their role.
With jests and jibes of playful bliss,
We love the sea, we cannot miss!

Reflections on Sand

In flip-flops I trudge, what a sight!
Crabs scurry past, giving me fright.
Sunburns and sunscreen, a comical fray,
Lobster legs dance while I stumble and sway.

Seagulls are laughing, they steal my fries,
I wheel around quickly, surprise in my eyes.
They're truly a menace, a feathered brigade,
As I wave my arms, like a beach-bound charade.

Voyage of the Current

Afloat on my raft, what a thrill,
I drink from my cooler—was that a spill?
The waves toss and turn, like a wild dance,
While I try to put on my best 'sailor' stance.

Mermaids are swimming, they give a wave,
I call out to join, feeling quite brave.
But they giggle and swim with a flick of their tails,
As I drift away, scouting for snails.

Mysteries of the Abyss

Diving down deep to find that glow,
A fish in a tuxedo, with nowhere to go!
He winks at me, speaks in a gurgling tone,
I nod, thinking he's just in love with my phone.

Octopus juggling, what a delight!
How did he learn to dance in the night?
I try to join in, but the tide pulls me back,
Leaving me flailing, what a fishy attack!

Harbor of Hope

The pier is a circus, so lively and bright,
With kids on their bicycles, laughing in flight.
Ice cream drips down, all over the floor,
While fishermen argue about turtles and lore.

A parrot on my shoulder, he squawks with flair,
As I sing to the waves, not a single care.
But the gulls just roll their eyes in disdain,
Maybe next time I'll practice in the rain!

Azure Embrace

In a world where fish wear hats,
Octopus juggles, how about that?
Crabs in tuxedos dance on the shore,
While seaweed whispers, "Give me more!"

Seahorses prance in a grand parade,
Trading tales of the mischief they made.
Starfish claps in a standing ovation,
For the jellyfish's quirky creation!

The gulls swoop in for a snack so slick,
While a clam decides to do a quick kick.
Splashing about with giggles galore,
Who knew sea life could be such a chore?

Floating along with a smile so wide,
While a dolphin jokes, "You really can't hide!"
In this watery world where laughter's the key,
It's a wacky, wild, fun jubilee!

Whispering Waves

Waves were gossiping, oh so loud,
Bubbles popping, a frothy crowd.
A fish in a bowtie sings a tune,
While turtles glide and do the moon.

Sea cucumbers are on a roll,
Fishes too busy taking a stroll.
"Don't be a grouper!" a shrimp yells bright,
As crabs crack jokes in the morning light.

Inky squids paint with colors bold,
Making masterpieces to behold.
But the starfish just snores in the sand,
Dreaming of a rock band so grand!

With sea glass shimmers, laughter and cheer,
Bubbles float by, oh dear, oh dear!
The glory of marine life's funny ways,
Bringing joy through the silly waves!

Serenity Below

In the depths where the sun's rays peek,
Fish are chatting—who would've thought they'd speak?
Anemones waving, "Pick me, oh please!"
While clownfish joke, "Swim with such ease!"

Corals are blushing in green and pink,
While shrimps wear sunglasses—"What do you think?"
A pufferfish jokes, "I've got no wiggle,"
And all the sea urchins laugh till they giggle.

The lobsters argue about who's the best,
While a stingray takes a rather bold rest.
In this kingdom of glee and marine flair,
Laughter bubbles up in the salty air!

So swim with the current, lose track of time,
In this whimsical world—everything's fine.
Serenity reigns, but the giggles don't stop,
Together we dance, as we flip and plop!

Echoes of the Deep

Fishy friends as they gather near,
Eels telling stories that we all cheer.
Wisdom from whales when they send out calls,
And a sunken treasure found by the squalls!

A clam with a pearl thinks she's quite grand,
But the barnacles giggle, all made of sand.
"Funny you think you're the belle of the ball,
We're just too stuck to take a nice fall!"

Mermaids giggle, flipping their hair,
While a crab tries to dance without a care.
Tangled in seaweed, he tumbles around,
As bubbles surround him, laughter resounds!

The dance of the deep, with a slap and a splash,
Where silliness reigns in a magnificent crash.
Underwater echoes, a comical spree,
Join the fun-fest—it's the place to be!

www.ingramcontent.com/pod-product-compliance
Lightning Source LLC
Chambersburg PA
CBHW072218070526
44585CB00015B/1387